HEADLINES

Conceived and produced by Weldon Owen Pty Ltd
59-61 Victoria Street, McMahons Point
Sydney, NSW 2060, Australia
Copyright © 2010 Weldon Owen Pty Ltd
First printed 2010

WELDON OWEN PTY LTD
Chief Executive Officer Sheena Coupe
Creative Director Sue Burk

Senior Vice President, International Sales Stuart Laurence
Sales Manager: United States Ellen Towell
Vice President, Sales: Asia and Latin America Dawn L. Owen
Administration Manager, International Sales Kristine Ravn
Production Director Todd Rechner
Production Controller Lisa Conway
Production Coordinator Mike Crowton
Production Assistant Nathan Grice

Concept Design Arthur Brown/Cooling Brown
Project Editor Jasmine Parker
Designer Colin Wheatland
Cartography Will Pringle, Mapgraphx
Art Manager Trucie Henderson
Picture Research Joanna Collard
Copy Editor Shan Wolody

Index Jo Rudd

ISBN 978-1-74252-132-9

Printed by Toppan Leefung Printing Limited
Manufactured in China

10 9 8 7 6 5 4 3 2 1

The paper used in the manufacture of this book is sourced from
wood grown in sustainable forests. It complies with the
Environmental Management System Standard ISO 14001:2004

A WELDON OWEN PRODUCTION

About the Author
Philip Wilkinson enjoys writing and talking about history,
architecture and the arts. His many books include the
award-winning *Amazing Buildings*, the United-Nations-endorsed
A Celebration of the Customs and Rituals of the World and the
best-selling *What the Romans Did For Us*. He lives in the Cotswolds
(England) and southern Bohemia (Czech Republic).

HEADLINES

Philip Wilkinson

WELDON
OWEN

Contents

TITANIC

WORLD WAR I

HINDENBURG

WORLD WAR II

MAN ON THE MOON

THE BERLIN WALL

INDIAN OCEAN TSUNAMI

The Biggest and the Best

Titanic

Designed like an ocean-going palace, *Titanic* was the biggest, most luxurious passenger ship of its time. When it was completed in 1912, there was no air travel and everyone who wanted to travel long distances had to go by sea. The major shipping companies, such as Cunard and the White Star Line, competed to provide safe, comfortable transport. *Titanic* was part of the White Star Line and was bigger than Cunard's largest vessels. It was 269 metres (883 ft) in length—longer than 11 tennis courts.

Titanic was constructed in Belfast, Ireland.

Gymnasium *The gymnasium w to women in the mornings and r in the afternoons. Exercise equip such as these cycles, was new fo*

First-class dining room
The first-class passengers ate their meals in a huge, elegant dining room. Dinner here consisted of a long meal of at least six courses, with some of the most expensive wines available.

Building *Titanic*
Construction took place at the Harland and Wolff shipyard in Belfast, Ireland. It took three years and around 3,000 workers.

Watertight design
The liner was divided into 16 sections, separated by walls called bulkheads. Each section was supposed to be watertight, so if water got into one or two sections, it would not flood the rest of the ship.

Bulkhead

THE UNSINKABLE SHIP

When *Titanic's* 1,343 passengers began their voyage across the Atlantic they were hoping for the journey of their lives. Some were on a one-way trip to start a new life in America; others were looking forward to a luxury vacation on board a ship they thought was unsinkable.

Steel hull *The hull was made of huge steel plates held together with some 3 million rivets.*

Second-class staterooms

Second-class dining room

Steam engines
A ship as large as Titanic *needed three engines. Two steam engines, each the size of a house, drove the port and starboard propellers. A smaller, more modern, engine drove the centre propeller.*

Main g or kit

First class   Second class   Third class

ss areas The classes were separated on board, the second and third classes on lower decks the first. This meant that when *Titanic* hit the erg, the first-class passengers could get to the oats more quickly.

First-class aterooms

Third-class berths

rd-class ing area

d-class hen

Luxury liner
The ship was packed with luxurious facilities such as a swimming pool, gym, Turkish bath and libraries, and her main rooms were decorated with rich wooden panelling.

Grand staircase *A broad staircase linked the levels of the first-class accommodation. It was decorated with carvings and paintings and had lights supported by bronze cherubs. A large glass dome let in natural light.*

The Voyage and the Crew

Titanic was designed for the popular route between Britain and the USA, a voyage scheduled to take about six days. Aft leaving the port of Southampton on Britain's southern coast the ship stopped at Cherbourg, France, and Queenstown, Irela to pick up more passengers before heading across the Atlant Ocean towards New York. Under the command of Captain Edward John Smith the vessel carried a crew of 899 men and women. As well as the officers, navigators and stokers who ke *Titanic* going, there were chefs, barbers, carpenters and all ki of other specialists to look after the passengers.

Edward John Smith

Harold Lowe

The officers
The ship's captain wa Edward John Smith, a very experienced officer who had wor for the White Star Li since 1880. Under hi command were seve ship's officers, inclu Fifth Officer Harold Lowe, who helped hi sail and run the vess

NORTH
AMERICA

14 April 1912, 11:40 pm,
Titanic *hit the iceberg.*

New York

At about 2:20 am the ship sank.

A T L A N T I C

O C E A N

Size comparison At 269 metres (883 ft) long, *Titanic* was almost four times the length of the modern Airbus A380 airliner and about three-quarters the length of today's biggest cruise ship, *Queen Mary 2*.

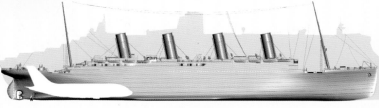

Airbus A380   R.M.S. *Titanic*   *Queen Mary 2*

...anic departure

...ce clear of the Irish coast, the
...o made good progress on the
...g journey across the Atlantic.
...me people thought, but this is
...t speculation, that the captain
...d been encouraged to sail
...ckly and beat the record
...an Atlantic crossing.

Southampton

Queenstown
(Cork)

Cherbourg

E U R O P E

...board music *Titanic* had two groups
...musicians: a five-person band who played
...certs and a trio who played in a reception
...m outside the first-class restaurant. The
...dleader, Wallace Hartley, gathered the two
...ups together to calm the passengers by
...ying as the ship sank. All eight musicians
...t their lives in the disaster.

...he bandleader

Class distinction
Like all liners of the time,
Titanic divided passengers
into three classes. First-
class passengers paid
more, and enjoyed more
luxurious accommodation,
better facilities and finer
food than those offered
to the other classes.

First-class   Third-class
passenger   passenger

The Sinking of R.M.S. *Titanic*

Late on the night of 14 April, when *Titanic* was about 724 kilometres (450 mi) away from New York, it ran into an iceberg. As the ship moved, the iceberg hit its hull in several places, water poured in, and soon the vessel's forward end was dipping dramatically towards the sea floor—*Titanic* was sinking. The radio operators sent out a distress signal, but no one close enough to come to the rescue heard the message. The crew launched the lifeboats, but there were not enough boats for everyone and 1,517 people perished in icy water.

Headline news The sinking of *Titanic* quickly made front-page news. People stopped in the street to read about the tragedy.

Sinking in stages

The bow of the ship went down first. To begin with, people thought the vessel would not sink and were reluctant to get into the lifeboats. But soon the hull started to break up and in just three hours the entire ship had sunk.

Water enters rips along the hull.   The bow s

Disaster strikes *When Titanic struck the iceberg, the hull quickly began to fill with water and the ship was pulled, bow first, below the waves. Women and children were helped to safety first because this was the custom of the time. There were not enough lifeboats for everyone on board.*

Flooding the bulkheads The ship was meant to stay afloat with up to four of its compartments full of water, but five of *Titanic's* sections filled up. This pulled the ship down, dragging the tops of the watertight bulkheads below the surface of the sea, so that even more compartments were filled.

> "We place absolute confidence in the *Titanic*. We believe the boat is unsinkable."
>
> PHILIP FRANKLIN, VICE PRESIDENT, THE WHITE STAR LINE

The hull breaks apart.

Titanic finally sinks.

Hidden mass Typically, about one-tenth of an iceberg is above the water level with the remaining nine-tenths hidden below. This makes icebergs hard to see, especially when rough waves conceal the upper part, as may have happened on *Titanic's* voyage.

Titanic Treasures

The wreck of *Titanic* was lost at the bottom of the Atlantic until an expedition led by Frenchman Jean-Louis Michel and American Robert Ballard found the hull 3.7 kilometres (2.3 mi) below the water surface in 1985. Archaeologists studied the wreck to find out how it broke up and around 6,000 objects from the ship have been brought to the surface. Among this treasure are gold and diamond jewellery, silverware, porcelain and all kinds of personal objects from clothing to letters and banknotes. These items paint a picture of life on board this luxury liner.

Titanic wreck
Robert Ballard found the wreck off Newfoundland, Canada. He and his team used a small submersible to explore it. They discovered that the ship's hull had broken in two, but much of the vessel was still intact.

Golden treasure
Items from the wreck include valuable jewellery, such as this gold nugget necklace. It may have belonged to Molly Brown, a passenger from Colorado, USA, who survived the sinking and insisted her lifeboat return to save more survivors.

Binoculars
This is one of the many personal possessions removed from *Titanic*. Some people think that the wreck and its contents should be treated as a grave and left alone.

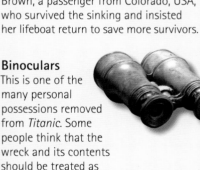

Delicate debris Surrounding the wreck was a large debris field with pieces of the ship, furniture, personal items and dinnerware—including these china plates. The wreck and its contents were scattered over 2.6 square kilometres (1 mi²).

Turning Point

After the sinking, the world's shipping companies and governments did what they could to prevent such a terrible disaster happening again. They moved shipping lanes further south, away from most of the icebergs, and ordered all ships to keep a 24-hour radio watch, so that they could pick up distress signals. Vessels had to carry enough lifeboats for all passengers and crew, and an International Ice Patrol was set up in 1914 to track icebergs and to warn ships. The seas were much safer as a result of all these measures.

LIFEBOATS

After the *Titanic* disaster, most shipping companies fitted extra lifeboats immediately. In addition, shipping regulations were changed so that all liners had to have enough lifeboats to accommodate all passengers and crew in an emergency.

INTERNATIONAL ICE PATROL

At first, the International Ice Patrol used boats sailing along main shipping lanes to look for ice hazards and icebergs. After World War II, they also used aeroplanes.

International Ice Patrol badge

NASA'S ICEBERG TRACKING

The USA's space agency, NASA, uses satellites to track icebergs. This image shows the Antarctic Larsen B Ice Shelf, whose 3,250 square kilometres (1,255 mi²) of ice collapsed in 2002, creating many icebergs.

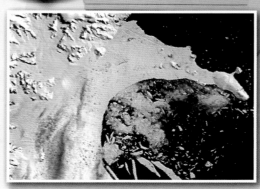

World War I

Franz Ferdinand was assassinated in Sarajevo, Bosnia.

On 28 June 1914, Archduke Franz Ferdinand of Austria, heir to the throne of the Austro-Hungarian Empire, visited Sarajevo, Bosnia, with his wife Sophie. As the couple rode through the streets in their open-topped car, they were shot dead by Gavrilo Princip, a Serb from Bosnia. Franz Ferdinand's family ruled a huge empire, covering the southern Slavic countries—Serbia, Bosnia and Croatia—as well as Austria, Hungary, Romania and the Czech lands. Some people, including Princip, wanted independence for the southern Slavic countries, but his murderous act caused the Empire to declare war on Serbia, starting one of the most terrible conflicts the world has ever seen.

THE ASSASSINATION

When Princip saw the Archduke's car coming towards him, he pulled out his gun and fired twice. His first shot hit the Archduke in the neck. The second hit the Duchess, who had instinctively thrown herself in front of her husband to protect him. One witness heard the Archduke say to her, "Sophie, Sophie, don't die. Live for our children."

Black Hand The Black Hand group was a secret society that tried to win freedom for the southern Slavic peoples by means of violence. It is thought that the group may have been behind the killing, supplying Princip and his comrades with weapons.

The plan Several would-be assassins lined the route of the Archduke's car but when one threw a grenade, it hit another car, causing panic and injuries. The Archduke's car sped away and this made it impossible for the other conspirators to target it. Princip had given up when the car took a wrong turning and he saw his chance.

State funeral The dead couple lay in state at the Imperial Palace in Vienna, so that people could pay their respects. They were then buried at Artstetten Castle in Lower Austria, their family's summer home.

The bloodied coat The first bullet burst the Archduke's jugular vein, spreading blood across his clothes. Both victims died within minutes of the shooting.

Leaders and Alliances

GREAT BRITAIN

Britain entered the war as an ally of France and Russia. It was supported by its many colonies and dominions, from Canada to Australia.

FRANCE

Invaded by Germany, France became one of the main battlegrounds of the war.

RUSSIA

Russia fought on the side of the Allied Powers, but left the war in 1917 after the Russian Revolution.

USA

The USA entered the war in 1917, partly because US ships had been sunk by German submarines.

ITALY

In 1915, Italy joined the war on the side of the Allies.

War powers *After the assassination, nations took sides according to alliances had built up in previous years. Europe w quickly divided between the Central Pow (allies of the Austro-Hungarian Empire) and their opponents, the Allied Powers.*

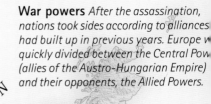

ATLANTIC OCEAN

Edinburgh

Belfast

IRELAND

Dublin

GREAT BRITAIN

London

Nor Se

NE

BELGIUM

Le Havre

Seine

Paris

Loire

N

FRANCE

Lyon

PORTUGAL

Douro

ANDORRA

Marseille

Madrid

Barcelona

SPAIN

Cor to F

Sardin to Ita

Balearic Islands
to Spain

M e d i t

Spanish Morocco

Morocco
to France

Algeria
to France

War leaders The political leaders of the time, such as the British and French prime ministers, the German emperor and the US president, took responsibility for declaring war and played key roles in drawing up the terms of peace in 1918.

H.H. Asquith

David Lloyd Geo

NORWAY

SWEDEN

FINLAND

Oslo

Helsinki

Stockholm

Leningrad
(St. Petersburg)

ARK
Copenhagen

Baltic Sea

mburg

East
Prussia

Minsk

RUSSIAN
EMPIRE

Berlin

Warsaw

RMANY

Dresden

Poland

Kiev

Prague

Ukraine

unich

Vienna

Budapest

Odessa

TENSTEIN

AUSTRIA-HUNGARY

Zagreb

SAN
ARINO

Sarajevo

ROMANIA

Bucharest

Danube

Black
Sea

Adriatic Sea

SERBIA

BULGARIA

ITALY

MONT.

Sofia

ome

ALBANIA

Constantinople

Naples

TURKEY

GREECE

Aegean Sea

Athens

Sicily

n   e   a   n   S   e   a

Crete

Malta

GERMANY
The Germans, supporting the Austro-Hungarian Empire, invaded Belgium and France, and became leading participants in the war.

AUSTRIA-HUNGARY
The Austro-Hungarians responded to the assassination by invading Serbia, beginning the war.

OTTOMAN EMPIRE
After secretly making an alliance with Germany in 1914, the Ottoman Empire—based in Turkey—joined the Central Powers.

World War I, 1914–1917
Allied Powers
Central Powers
Neutral nations

0   250 miles
0   250 km

eorges Clemenceau

Woodrow Wilson

Kaiser Wilhelm II

17

Battles and Warfare

The war lasted more than four years, from 28 July 1914 to 11 November 1918. Fighting spread to many parts of the wor with bitter trench warfare and the use of poison gas and fla throwers. Aircraft were used in warfare for the first time and in 1916, the first tanks appeared on the battlefield, wreaking destruction with their guns. Millions were killed in the fighti and finally Germany and its allies were defeated. The oppone made a treaty—signed at the palace of Versailles in France—wh severely limited Germany's power and territory.

War zone The two main European lines of fighting were the Western and Eastern Fronts. Most of the trench warfare took place on the Western Front while the fighting in the east involved freer troop movements.

Allied Powers	Major battles	Western Front
Central Powers	Allied offensives	Farthest advances of Central Powers
Neutral nations	Central Powers offensives	Stabilised front

Uniforms
Soldiers on both sides wore uniforms that indicated each person's rank, so that the chain of command was clear, and identified who was on which side in the confusing conditions of battle.

British soldier

German soldier

THE TRENCHES

Much of the fighting on land consisted of trench warfare. Armies dug and occupied lines of trenches facing one another. Then one side would attempt to capture the other's trench by going "over the top"—attacking their rivals and trying to push them back. Conditions in the cramped, muddy trenches were appalling and millions died in these battles.

At sea The Allies had large navies and tried to stop the movement of German ships, cutting off food and other supplies from reaching central Europe. This strategy was often successful, but the Central Powers sank many Allied ships with their submarines.

TIMELINE BATTLES

1914	1914	1914	1914	1914	1915	1916	1916	1916
1 Tannenberg	**2** Masurian Lakes	**3** Lemberg	**4** Marne .	**5** Ypres	**6** Gallipoli	**7** Verdun	**8** Jutland	**9** Somme

Wartime Roles

When war came, industries concentrated on making supplies for the armed forces and there were shortages of food and other goods at home as a result. Millions of men went off to fight and the women and children who were left at home had to survive on rationed food. Many women had to take over the factory jobs of the absent men; others became nurses. Before 1914, most women had stayed at home to look after their families and paid work was a new experience for many. Although the work was hard, it gave women a new confidence and independence.

Animals Even animals were involved in the war. Dogs were trained to run through the complex networks of trenches carrying messages. They could travel faster than humans and were smaller targets for enemy riflemen.

For
EVERY
FIGHTER
a
WOMAN
WORKER

UNITED
WAR
WORK
CAMPAIGN

CARE
for
HER
through The YWCA

Women Posters encouraged women to go to work to support the war effort. Some worked on farms and in food production, others joined munitions factories, made uniforms for the troops or trained to become nurses.

Children Most countries had rules that forbade children from joining the army. In Britain, soldiers had to be 17 or older, but in places such as Russia, boys in their early teens took part in the war.

Turning Point

Commemorative stamp

The enormous casualties of World War I—some 10 million people were killed in action and many more injured—made the assassination of Franz Ferdinand one of the most terrible of history's turning points. After the war, the Austro-Hungarian Empire was broken up, giving many countries of central Europe independence, and the Treaty of Versailles took away Germany's colonies and limited the power of its army. People hoped that this would reduce the chance of another major war. But the limits placed on Germany's power caused resentment, which was one of the causes of World War II only 21 years later.

Russia 1,700,000
Germany 1,600,000
France 1,359,000
Austria–Hungary 922,000
Italy 689,000
Britain 658,700
Romania 335,706
Turkey 250,000
Bulgaria 87,500
USA 58,480

DEATH IN WAR

It is not know for sure how many people lost their lives in the war because many countries did not keep adequate records. Some estimates put the total figure at around 10 million military deaths and 6 million civilians.

FIELD HOSPITALS

Military hospitals were set up close to the battlefields to treat the wounded. Staff had to cope with extremely difficult conditions, from water shortages to lice infestations, but could treat patients quickly.

Treaty of Versailles

The fighting ended on 11 November 1918 with the victory of the Allied Powers. The following year, exactly five years after the assassination, Germany and the Allied leaders, including the French prime minister Georges Clemenceau, signed the Treaty of Versailles.

Hindenburg

Hindenburg was the king of the airships. At 245 metres (804 ft) long, it was more than three times the length of a Boeing 747. Most of the space inside was taken up with 16 vast containers of hydrogen that kept the craft in the air. Named after German president Paul von Hindenburg, the enormous craft was finished in 1936 and was designed to carry travellers across the Atlantic Ocean in under three days. Airships had been safe, successful passenger carriers since 1900, but in 1937 *Hindenburg* caught fire and dozens of passengers and crew were killed. This disaster brought the age of the airships to an end.

Hindenburg was built in Friedrichshafen, Germany.

Flight path
Hindenburg's *flight took it from Germany, over southern England and across the North Atlantic Ocean to the USA. The airship had made this journey several times before and also served on the route from Frankfurt to Rio de Janeiro.*

Rudder *The rudder was used to steer Hindenburg on its course through the air. It was operated by the pilot from the control car, which was at the front of the airship.*

Gas cell *Much of the structure was filled with 16 huge cotton gas bags. When the airship was ready to fly, these were filled with hydrogen, a gas that is lighter than air and so made the craft rise above the ground.*

Tail *The cross-shaped tail section gave the airship structural strength and also housed the rudder. Germany's ruling Nazi party was keen to use the airship for publicity and their swastika symbol was painted on the tail fins.*

Construction The airship was constructed in a huge hangar. Scaffolding supported the vast structure while the main framework, made of a lightweight metal alloy called duralumin, was put together. The airship's outer "skin" was made of cotton fabric.

Engines There were four 16-cylinder diesel engines, each slung in housings on either side of the airship. They could move the craft at up to 137 kilometres per hour (85 mph).

Engine operator and mechanic

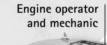

Pro

Internal workings of engine

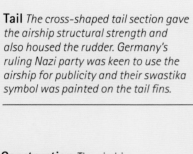

The airship was designed to carry passengers—especially on long journeys, such as crossing the Atlantic—more quickly than an ocean liner. Its huge size allowed it to carry a vast amount of hydrogen, giving the craft plenty of lifting power to carry heavy loads. Even so, fewer than 100 people were travelling on *Hindenburg* on its final journey.

Outer skin *The fabric covering of the airship was painted with a silver varnish. This was meant to protect the ship from damage by infrared and ultraviolet rays, but the varnish also contained aluminium powder, which made it explosive.*

Inner frame *The frame consisted of wheel-like structures, built from duralumin, a light but strong aluminium alloy containing copper, silicon, magnesium and manganese.*

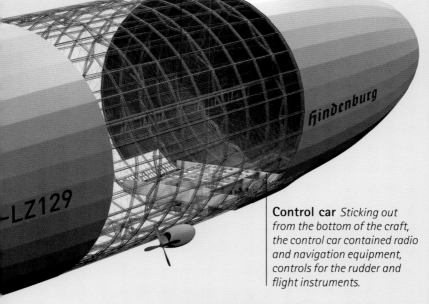

Control car *Sticking out from the bottom of the craft, the control car contained radio and navigation equipment, controls for the rudder and flight instruments.*

Passenger decks Passengers spent the journey on two decks behind the control car. The public areas included a lounge and dining room. Each tiny cabin contained bunk beds and a chair.

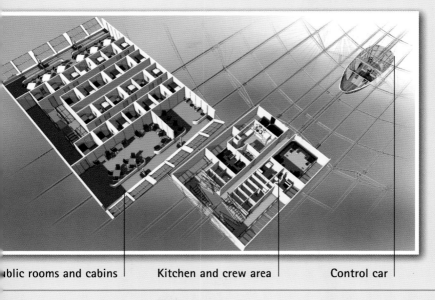

| Public rooms and cabins | Kitchen and crew area | Control car |

Postcards from the air

The Zeppelin Company promoted *Hindenburg* by selling postcards showing its luxury viewing deck. The pilot would fly as low as was safe, to give passengers the best possible view

ver New York *Hindenburg* sped
st ocean liners, outran trains,
nained airborne for days or
eks without refuelling and had
ephones, electric lights and two
nes of fuel on board.

LZ129

THE JOURNEY

On 3 May 1937, *Hindenburg* set off from
Frankfurt, Germany, for the 60-hour
journey across the Atlantic Ocean to
Lakehurst, New Jersey. There were only
36 passengers, but the airship carried
a large crew of 61, which included a
number of trainees. The passengers
enjoyed the luxurious facilities offered on
the trip, which included a library, lounge,
smoking room and promenades with
big windows from which people could
admire the view. Passengers also liked the
airship because it was faster and cheaper
than an ocean liner, the only other way
of travelling long distances at this time.

Interior design Murals and maps
decorated the luxurious public rooms,
such as the lounge and writing room.
Furniture was mostly made of
aluminium to keep down the weight.
Even the airship's grand piano was
made largely of an aluminium alloy.

The Day Disaster Struck

Identification button

There were strong headwinds on the journey and *Hindenburg* was several hours late arriving at Lakehurst. Storms made it unsafe to land, but finally the winds died down and Captain Max Pruss steered the craft towards the mooring mast. Witnesses on the ground reported seeing flames coming from the side of the airship and the hydrogen inside ignited. In less than a minute, the ship was engulfed in flames and 13 passengers, 22 crew and one member of the ground staff died.

Preparing to fly People gathered around *Hindenburg* to see off their friends as the airship prepared to take off on 3 May 1937. Although forecasters predicted strong headwinds that would slow the craft down, everyone expected that it would otherwise be a normal transatlantic flight.

Captured on film

When *Hindenburg* approached Lakehurst, New Jersey, around 12 hours later than scheduled, it was raining heavily. At 6:30 pm, as the airship floated down towards its moorings and with only 60 metres (180 ft) to go, a small wisp of flame appeared near its tail. In less than 40 seconds, the entire airship was engulfed in flames.

1 second

FROM THE SCENE OF THE DISASTER

Imagine standing on the tarmac, awaiting the landing of one of the most celebrated and luxurious aircraft ever to have existed—and then imagine witnessing it engulfed in flames, reduced to cinders in a matter of moments. Picture the shock and horror of the landing crew, standing ready to secure the airship to its mooring; the terror of the crew and passengers as they try to escape the flames. Herbert Morrison was a radio broadcaster sent to Lakehurst, New Jersey, to report back live on the landing. Little did he know that his broadcast was to report a tragic event. Within minutes, his story was radioed all around the world.

"It's burst into flames.
It's burst into flames
and it's ... It's falling.
It's crashing. Get out of the
way. Get out of the way
please. It's falling on
the mooring mast.
This is terrible ..."

HERBERT MORRISON—LIVE BROADCAST

conds

5 seconds

15 seconds

25 seconds

30 seconds

How Did it Happen?

No one knows for sure why the airship caught fire, but there are several theories. Some historians think *Hindenburg* was sabotaged by an enemy of Germany's Nazi rulers. Some believe that when lightning struck the airship it set alight some of the hydrogen that the ship was venting, starting the fire, while another theory suggests that sparks from one of the airship's backfiring engines caused the blaze. Scientists also disagree about how the fire spread, some blaming burning hydrogen, others pointing to the flammable paint with which the airship was covered.

The aftermath Four days after the crash, an inquiry was underway, ordered by the United States Department of Commerce and headed up by South Trimble Junior, a lawyer from Kentucky. The court began hearing the evidence.

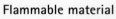

Flammable material
The varnish in the fabric from the airship's skin contained a chemical called acetone and particles of aluminium, both of which burn very easily.

International news Accounts of the tragic event, which killed 36 people, shocked the world. Before this, not a single life had been lost in a German airship. Now *Hindenburg*, the largest passenger-carrying vessel ever to fly, was a mass of twisted wreckage.

Turning Point

Although airships had carried passengers safely, when *Hindenburg* caught fire, people realised the risk of travelling beneath an enormous container full of flammable hydrogen. As a result, the age of passenger airships came to an end and people put more resources into building aeroplanes. Eventually jet airliners were developed that carried people across the globe at still greater speeds. A few smaller airships, generally filled with safer helium gas, are still used today, both for carrying passengers and for displaying advertisements.

MODERN AIRSHIPS

Today, two kinds of airships are used. Balloon-like, non-rigid designs are used in advertising and scientific research. Rigid craft—sometimes called dirigible, or steerable, airships—carry passengers, usually on short tourist flights.

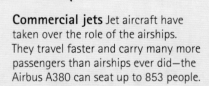

Jet engines At take-off, the A380's four jet engines produce more power than 3,500 family cars.

Commercial jets Jet aircraft have taken over the role of the airships. They travel faster and carry many more passengers than airships ever did—the Airbus A380 can seat up to 853 people.

FIGHTER JETS

The power of jet engines makes possible military aircraft that can fly faster than the speed of sound. At an altitude of 9,000 metres (30,000 ft) the F-22 Raptor fighter can cruise at 1,725 kilometres per hour (1,070 mph).

The Nazis invaded Poland on 1 September 1939.

World War II

Adolf Hitler Hitler was known for his fanatical, ranting speeches, which nevertheless had the power to move the German people and persuade them that Nazi views were valid.

On 1 September 1939, the German army invaded Poland, a drastic action that had its roots in events that took place 20 years before. In 1918, the treaty that ended World War I had severely limited the power, territory and army of the defeated Germans. This led to resentment in Germany, where things were made worse by huge economic hardship in the 1930s. The Germans then elected as their leader Adolf Hitler, a fanatical right-wing dictator obsessed with making Germany more powerful. Hitler invaded Czechoslovakia in 1938, and when he also took over Poland, the leaders of France and Great Britain realised they would have to use violence to stop him. They declared war on 3 September 1939.

Panzer tank Tough and reliable, Panzer tanks were used throughout the war by the German army, both to support foot soldiers and to power their way through the armoured vehicles and defences of the enemy.

Stuka dive bomber Designed to dive directly towards its target before dropping its bombs, the Junkers JU 87 Stuka was the most effective bomber at the beginning of the war. The Nazis used it widely while invading Poland and the Low Countries.

NAZIS INVADE POLAND

Soon after the Nazis invaded Poland from the north, west and south, troops from the USSR—who were allies of Germany at this time—swept into the country from the east. The Polish army was forced to withdraw and, although Poland did not formally surrender, Germany and the USSR took over the country's government. The Nazis celebrated with victory parades like this one.

Leaders and Alliances

GREAT BRITAIN
Britain fought throughout the war, both supporting the other Allies and preventing a Nazi invasion of its islands.

USA
The USA joined the war in 1941, after Japan bombed its base at Pearl Harbor. Its aircraft scored victories over Japan in the Pacific.

USSR
Despite the Germans and Russians signing a secret treaty, Germany invaded the USSR in June 1941, bringing it into the conflict.

Worldwide war
Gradually more countries joined the fighting, sometimes decisively changing the course of the war. They formed into two major military alliances. The Allies encompassed Great Britain, the USA and USSR. The Axis included Germany, Japan and Italy.

IRELAND
Belfast
Edinburgh
Dublin
GREAT
BRITAIN
London
North Sea
DENM
NETH.
Ha
BELGIUM
LUX.
G
Le Havre
Seine
Paris
Loire
ATLANTIC OCEAN
N
FRANCE
Lyon
Bern
SWITZ
Milan
Douro
ANDORRA
Marseille
MONAC
PORTUGAL
Madrid
SPAIN
Barcelona
Corsica
to France
Sardinia
to Italy
Balearic Islands
to Spain
Medit
Algeria
to France
Tunisia
to France
NORW

World War II, 1941 Europe
- Allies
- Axis
- Neutral
- Axis controlled

Leaders of war
The political leaders of the most powerful combatant countries controlled the broad strategy of the war in close collaboration with the heads of the armed forces.

Winston Churchill

F.D. Roosevelt

FINLAND

SWEDEN

Helsinki

Leningrad
(St. Petersburg)

Stockholm

ESTONIA

openhagen

Baltic Sea

LATVIA

LITHUANIA

East
Prussia
to Germany

Minsk

Moscow

USSR

Berlin

Warsaw

Dresden

POLAND

Kiev

Prague

CZECHOSLOVAKIA

Vienna

stria

Budapest

HUNGARY

Odessa

Zagreb

ROMANIA

*Black
Sea*

YUGOSLAVIA

Bucharest

Sarajevo

Danube

BULGARIA

Adriatic Sea

ALBANIA

Sofia

Constantinople

Naples

Aegean Sea

GREECE

Athens

TURKEY

Syria

Cyprus

Crete

Lebanon

ean Sea

250 miles

250 km

PALESTINE

NAZI GERMANY
Its strength worn down by the Allies—especially, after 1941, by the USSR—Germany was finally defeated in May 1945.

JAPAN
After entering the war against the Allies in 1941, Japan fought bitterly, only surrendering in August 1945.

ITALY
Under Fascist dictator Benito Mussolini, Italy entered the war on the Axis side in 1940.

Adolf Hitler

Benito Mussolini

Joseph Stalin

Battles and Warfare

In 1940, Germany's strategy of Blitzkrieg (lightning war) overwhelmed Belgium, Holland and France, but in the Battle of Britain, the British defeated Germany in the air, forcing Hitler to put off his plans to invade Britain. In the following year, Japan bombed the US base at Pearl Harbor, bringing the USA into the war. Between 1942 and 1944, the war was fought on several fronts—the Pacific, North Africa, the USSR and Europe. Gradually the power of the USA and USSR helped the Allies defeat Hitler by May 1945. Japan surrendered in August after atomic bombs were dropped on Hiroshima and Nagasaki

Theatres of War, WWII
- ⚡ Major battle
- → German attack

0   300 miles
0   300 km

Nazi conquests
In the early years, the Nazis conquered vast areas of Europe, moving westwards across Holland, Belgium and France, east into the USSR, north into Scandinavia and south towards Greece.

Atomic bomb
Japan fought on after the Nazis were defeated and the Americans, who had developed the atomic bomb, decided to use this weapon to force them to surrender.

Air warfare Among the most destructive weapons wielded by the Allies were bombers, such as the Avro Lancaster, which they used to destroy German cities and industrial targets. Lancaster crews flew more than 150,000 flight operations, or "sorties", against the enemy. Each aircraft was armed with eight machine guns and could carry bombs weighing up to 10,000 kilograms (22,000 lb).

TIMELINE OF BATTLES		2 *Siege of Leningrad*		4 *Stalingrad*		6 *Kursk*		8 *Philippine Sea*		10 *Okinawa*
	1941	1941–44	1941	1942–43	1942	1943	1944	1944	1944–45	1945
	1 *Operation Barbarossa*		3 *Pearl Harbor*		5 *Operation Torch*		7 *Normandy Landing*		9 *Battle of the Bulge*	

The Holocaust

The Nazis saw Germany as a "master race" whose destiny was to rule a vast empire. According to this belief system, the people stopping them doing this were the Jews, whom the Nazis persecuted mercilessly. Hitler proposed a "Final Solution" to this Jewish question, rounding up Jews and sending them—along with other perceived enemies, such as gypsies— to concentration camps, where, after living in appalling conditions, they were killed. This was the Holocaust, in which 6 million Jews and many others perished in Nazi death camps, such as Auschwitz and Treblinka in Poland.

Yellow star The Nazis forced Jewish people in Germany and German-occupied countries to wear a badge showing a yellow Star of David. Those wearing the badge were ruthlessly persecuted.

Shoes More than one million people, most of them Jews, were murdered at the huge Nazi concentration and extermination camp at Auschwitz. This pile contains some of the shoes left after they were killed.

No escape Two high fences topped with barbed wire surrounded the Auschwitz concentration camp. Any prisoner who tried to escape was instantly machine-gunned by the guards, who stood in watchtowers overlooking the fences.

Turning Point

Millions lost their lives during World War II—in the fighting, the Holocaust and the bombing of cities from Europe to Japan. No one wanted another war on such a terrible scale and, in 1945, the United Nations organisation was founded to encourage world peace and understanding. But the balance of power between nations after the war caused problems. Russia dominated eastern Europe, bringing oppressive communist rule to many countries and creating tense relations between the USA and USSR for some 40 years.

MILITARY EFFORTS

During the war, some armies occasionally still used horses in battle and for transport. After 1945, war became a more high-tech activity, with sophisticated weapons and aircraft and the terrible threat of nuclear weapons.

HOLOCAUST VICTIMS

The Hall of Names at Yad Vashem, Israel, is the Jewish people's memorial to the Jews who died in the Holocaust. The round ceiling in the main hall is covered with the photographs and pages of testimony of 600 of the victims.

USSR 20,600,000
China 10,000,000
Germany 6,850,000
Poland 6,123,000
Japan 2,000,000
Yugoslavia 1,706,000
France 810,000
Greece 520,000
USA 500,000
Austria 480,000

Loss of life
The huge numbers involved and the different ways of counting casualties make it impossible to say exactly how many people died in the war. The table shows estimates of casualties in the worst-hit countries.

Apollo 11 took off from Cape Canaveral, Florida.

Man on the Moon

In 1961, US President John F. Kennedy committed the USA to "landing a man on the Moon and returning him safely to the Earth". After several Apollo mission flights, the team at the US space agency, NASA, was ready, and their Apollo 11 craft was launched from the space centre near Cape Canaveral, Florida, on 16 July 1969. Three astronauts were aboard: mission commander Neil Alden Armstrong, lunar module pilot Edwin Eugene "Buzz" Aldrin and command module pilot Michael Collins. All three had been on space flights before, but everyone knew their mission was dangerous and risky.

All around the world, millions watched as the astronauts landed on the Moon and safely piloted their craft home.

Control panel The Command Module's control panel had 24 instruments, 566 switches and a tiny computer with less computing power than a modern mobile phone. With these basic resources, the astronauts were able to fly 384,403 kilometres (238,857 mi) to the Moon and back.

Engine nozzle *The main engine at the rear of the Command Module was fired when entering and leaving lunar orbit and was also used occasionally to make small adjustments to the spacecraft's course.*

Lift off On 16 July 1969 the Saturn rocket's huge engines roared and the Apollo 11 flight began. The rocket's great power was needed to propel the spacecraft so that it could break free of Earth's gravity.

Viewing ticket Special tickets issued by NASA gave access to the VIP viewing area at Cape Canaveral. People kept these as cherished souvenirs of the launch.

JOHN F. KENNEDY SPACE CENTER

APOLLO 11

№ 6306

The National Aeronautics and Space Administration cordially welcomes you to the launch of Apollo 11, the first mission planned to land Man on the Moon and return him safely to Earth.

Kurt H. Debus, Director
Kennedy Space Center, NASA

This credential is issued to the bearer for his sole, exclusive, personal use, and is not transferable. After launch, it may be kept as a souvenir of the mission.

Antenna *The four-dish antenna enabled the astronauts to communicate by radio with Mission Control on Earth.*

Access tunnel *This linked the Command Module with the Lunar Module, the section of the Apollo craft that landed on the Moon.*

Service Module *The cylinder-shaped Service Module held large tanks of fuel for the engines plus containers of oxygen to enable the astronauts to breathe in the airless conditions of space.*

Command Module *This was where the astronauts lived during their journey to the Moon. It was the only part of the spacecraft that made the full journey back to Earth.*

APOLLO 11

The flight to the Moon and the return journey each took three days. The three astronauts spent most of this time in the Command Module, where they ate and worked. They had a lot to do—flying the craft and preparing for landing— so slept only about five hours a day. The Command Module was very cramped, but in the weightless conditions of space the men could float around the small craft, finding room to stretch out.

The Space Race

Sputnik The first man-made object to orbit Earth was the tiny Russian satellite, Sputnik 1, which was launched in October 1957. The larger Sputnik 2 followed a month later.

Vostok 1 Gagarin's spacecraft was the first of six one-person craft named Vostok ("east" in Russian). Gagarin flew in a spherical capsule in front of a rocket section containing the engines.

In the 1950s and 1960s, the USA and USSR (Russia) were the world's most powerful nations. Their rivalry to be the most advanced in space exploration became known as the "space race". In 1949, the Americans began to send monkeys into space, but the space race began in earnest in 1957, when the USSR launched the first satellite. The first man in space, Yuri Gagarin, and the first woman, Valentina Tereshkova, were also Russians. With the Apollo 11 flight, the USA won the race to put a human being on the Moon, but the Russians scored successes with several unmanned flights to the Moon.

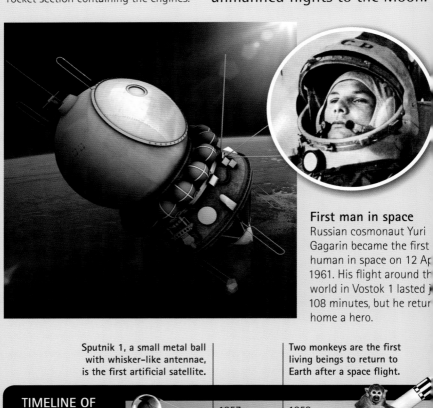

First man in space
Russian cosmonaut Yuri Gagarin became the first human in space on 12 Apr 1961. His flight around th world in Vostok 1 lasted j 108 minutes, but he retur home a hero.

Sputnik 1, a small metal ball with whisker-like antennae, is the first artificial satellite.

Two monkeys are the first living beings to return to Earth after a space flight.

TIMELINE OF SPACE TRAVEL

| | 1957 | 1959 |

First woman in space

Cosmonaut Valentina Tereshkova was the first woman in space. After rigorous training, she was selected personally for her mission by the USSR's leader Nikita Khrushchev. In June 1963, she made 48 orbits of Earth in her spacecraft, Vostok 6.

View of Earth

The Apollo 11 astronauts took the first photographs of Earth rising over the Moon. In this image, the North Pole is on the right and the brown landmass towards the left is Australia.

First to the Moon

As the first astronauts to land on the Moon, the crew of Apollo 11, especially Neil Armstrong and Buzz Aldrin, became world famous. Their portraits appeared on countless souvenirs, in newspapers and magazines.

The Russian Yuri Gagarin becomes the first human to fly into space.

Apollo 11 astronauts land successfully on the Moon.

1961

1969

First Man on the Moon

When Apollo 11 was orbiting the Moon, the astronauts separated the spacecraft into two sections. The Command Module stayed in lunar orbit and the Lunar Module touched down safely on the Moon at 9:56 pm Eastern Daylight Time on 20 July 1969. First Armstrong, then Aldrin, climbed down the ladder and stepped onto the Moon's surface. They found it covered with fine, powder-like dust.

Live on TV A small television camera mounted on the outside of the Lunar Module recorded Neil Armstrong's first steps on the Moon. Although the pictures were blurred, they thrilled millions of people around the world.

Lunar Module This was designed to land on the Moon surface. It was in two parts—the descent stage and the ascent stage. When Armstrong and Aldrin left the Moon, they took off in the ascent stage, leaving the descent stage behind.

Ladder *The astronauts climbed down to the lunar surface using this ladder. It was so light that it would have collapsed under the weight of an astronaut on Earth, but was strong enough for the weightless conditions on the Moon.*

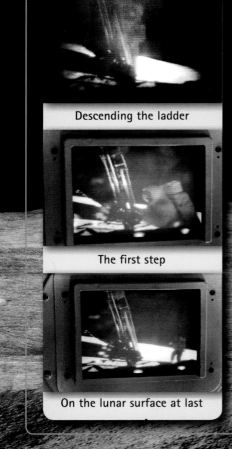

Descending the ladder

The first step

On the lunar surface at last

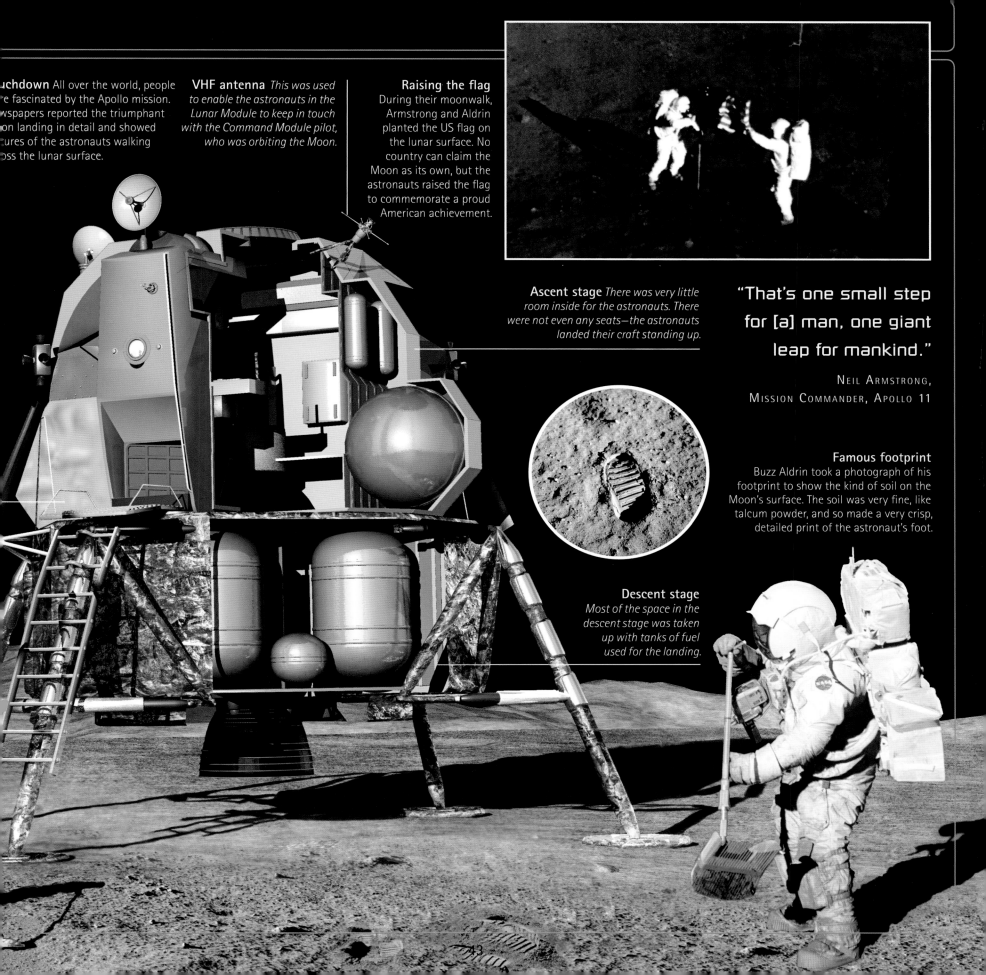

uchdown All over the world, people re fascinated by the Apollo mission. wspapers reported the triumphant on landing in detail and showed ures of the astronauts walking ss the lunar surface.

VHF antenna *This was used to enable the astronauts in the Lunar Module to keep in touch with the Command Module pilot, who was orbiting the Moon.*

Raising the flag
During their moonwalk, Armstrong and Aldrin planted the US flag on the lunar surface. No country can claim the Moon as its own, but the astronauts raised the flag to commemorate a proud American achievement.

Ascent stage *There was very little room inside for the astronauts. There were not even any seats—the astronauts landed their craft standing up.*

"That's one small step for [a] man, one giant leap for mankind."

NEIL ARMSTRONG, MISSION COMMANDER, APOLLO 11

Famous footprint
Buzz Aldrin took a photograph of his footprint to show the kind of soil on the Moon's surface. The soil was very fine, like talcum powder, and so made a very crisp, detailed print of the astronaut's foot.

Descent stage
Most of the space in the descent stage was taken up with tanks of fuel used for the landing.

43

Research on the Moon

During their short time on the Moon, the astronauts carried out various experiments. They collected samples to bring back to Earth: a number of rocks, some of the powdery soil and two "cores", or tubes, containing material from up to 13 centimetres (5 in) beneath the Moon's surface. They also left scientific equipment on the Moon that could be monitored from Earth. This equipment had several roles: to detect "moonquakes", thus helping scientists to understand the geology of the Moon, to study the effects of "moon dust" and to measure precisely the distance between the Moon and Earth.

Glove guidelines The astronauts did not have much time on the Moon, so Neil Armstrong kept a list on his glove of all the tasks that he had to perform during the moonwalk, which lasted roughly 2 hours, 30 minutes.

Carrying out experiments
Buzz Aldrin carried two experiment packages off the Lunar Module. Although the equipment was bulky, he found it easy to move in lunar gravity, which is one-sixth of Earth's.

Sample collection
As well as collecting rock samples, the astronauts set up three experiments: a reflector to bounce laser beams back to Earth, a collector to gather solar particles and a seismometer to measure moonquakes.

Turning Point

The Apollo 11 mission was a triumph, showing not just the skill and bravery of the three astronauts but also the research and hard work of a vast team of scientists, engineers and other experts. It was followed up by five further human journeys to the Moon. NASA then used its expertise to concentrate on less risky unmanned space probes, on developing reusable craft—the Space Shuttle—and on building the International Space Station, where scientists could live and work in space for long periods.

FUTURE EXPLORATION

On later expeditions to the Moon, astronauts took battery-powered lunar rovers in the Lunar Module and used these vehicles to travel further across the surface, examining craters, mountains and other features.

INTERNATIONAL SPACE STATION

A huge laboratory in space built by 16 countries, the International Space Station orbits Earth carrying a crew of seven astronauts. Their work has already told us a lot about what it is like to live in space and how to build structures there.

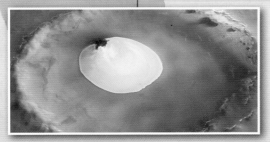

Ice on Mars Since 2003, Mars Express has orbited Mars, taking photographs, mapping the planet and doing experiments. A number of photographs show ice on the planet's surface and some think Mars may once have been home to some kind of life.

The Berlin Wall

The flag of the German Democratic Republic

The Berlin Wall was in Germany.

After World War II, Germany was divided into two countries, the capitalist Federal Republic of Germany in the West and the communist German Democratic Republic (GDR) in the East. The city of Berlin was in the East, but was also divided between the two countries. Many people in the East hated the totalitarian communist regime and escaped to the West through Berlin. So in 1961, the GDR began building a 155-kilometre (96-mi) concrete wall all the way around West Berlin, preventing people leaving East Berlin without permission. The wall became a symbol for the way all the communist states of eastern and central Europe curtailed the freedom of their people.

West Berlin

Staaken
Chausseestraße
Heerstraße
Invalidenstraße
Bornholmer Straße
Prinzenstraße
Checkpoint Charlie (Friedrichstraße)
Oberbaumbrücke
Sonnenallee
Checkpoint Bravo (Dreilinden)
East Berlin
Griebnitzsee
Waltersdorfer Chaussee

● Allied checkpoints
● East German checkpoints

Checkpoints

There were eight border crossings along the wall that separated East and West Berlin. Westerners could visit East Berlin; East Berliners with official permission could enter West Berlin.

Germany after World War II

Four Allied countries took control of Germany to rebuild it after the war. The USSR occupied the eastern zone; France, Britain and the USA controlled the western.

THE BERLIN WALL

The wall was a huge double concrete barrier surrounding West Berlin and cutting it off from East Germany. Watching over the wall were armed guards in more than 100 watchtowers. Barbed wire, extra mesh fences, guard dogs and anti-vehicle trenches made it almost impossible for East Germans to escape to West Berlin.

Church of St Elizabeth
Most of the buildi were cleared from Death Strip, but o the 19th-century church of St Elizab with a tall Gothic s was left stranded between the two parallel walls.

Concrete wall
The wall was made of solid concrete blocks that were too strong to knock down with a truck or bulldozer.

Mesh fence w built-in ala

Life behind the wall The people of East Berlin got used to living next to a towering barrier that prevented nearly all of them travelling to the West. Some, whose houses were knocked down to make way for the wall, were forced to move.

Building the wall

The wall began as a wire fence, but this was later replaced with a much stronger barrier made of concrete. This material was chosen because the large blocks could be laid quickly and were very strong.

Flood lighting

Watchtower

Tall watchtowers gave the guards a good view over a long stretch of the wall and the Death Strip. Strong lighting helped them to see the whole area at night.

Failed escape

East Berliners who tried to escape over the wall, such as Bernd Sievert in 1971, were usually shot dead by the guards. This photograph shows guards in the Death Strip taking away Sievert's body.

Barbed wire

...ew who managed ...cale the wall were ...aced with another ...tacle in the Death ...p—coils of barbed ...This slowed people ...own, allowing the ...rds to aim and fire.

The Death Strip

The empty space between the two walls was covered with gravel, so anyone running across it would make a noise. If a successful escapee left footprints in the gravel, the nearby guards were punished.

Keeping Control

Lucky escape Frieda Schulze had an apartment overlooking the border and escaped out of her window. An East German policeman tried to pull her back into the building, but West Germans outside successfully helped her to safety.

For most people, life in the GDR was bad. There were food shortages, poor facilities and no freedom of speech. Anyone who spoke out against the state was punished—they could lose their job or go to prison, where they might be tortured. Many people longed to escape to the West. The government's Ministry for State Security, known as the Stasi, was a secret police organisation designed to silence objectors and prevent escapes. Using networks of spies, informers and listening devices, they tracked down dissidents and treated them ruthlessly. Many who tried to escape across the wall were simply shot.

Watchtower
Guards in the watchtowers had good view of the prison and land around.

Stasi chief

As Minister for State Security, Erich Mielke was head of the Stasi from 1957 until 1989. His 85,000 full-time employees spied on the people of the GDR and harassed anyone who did not agree with the communist regime.

Prison cell Most of the people held in the Hohenschönhausen prison had not been sentenced. Many were imprisoned for their political beliefs; some were people who had tried to escape over the Berlin Wall.

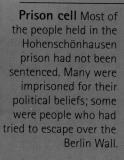

Guards

The prison was in a restricted area and armed guards patrolled the walls.

Hohenschönhausen prison

The Stasi used this prison in Berlin to hold prisoners who had been detained because of information received from their network of spies. The building is now a museum.

The Wall Comes Down

Communist leader
Erich Honecker oversaw the building of the wall in 1961, and led the GDR from 1976. He resigned in 1989, shortly before the wall came down.

Demonstration One of the largest demonstrations against the communist regime in East Germany took place on 4 November 1989, when thousands of people gathered in Alexanderplatz.

By 1989, so many people wanted to leave the communist countries of Europe that some states, including Hungary and Czechoslovakia, were forced to open up their borders and some East Germans escaped to the West through these countries. Then in September 1989, people began to protest on the streets of Berlin in increasing numbers. By early November, the East German government bowed to the pressure and announced that people would be able to leave for the West. On 9 November, thousands crossed through the gates in the wall. Soon they were bringing hammers and pickaxes to begin knocking down the wall.

On 9 November, the East German authorities finally allowed people to cross the wall. On the next day, all the border guards could do was to observe, and later that morning people began to pull the wall down.

...during barrier

...its various forms, from wire ...nce to fortified double concrete ...rrier, the Berlin Wall stood for ...me 28 years. Because movement ...ough the wall's checkpoints was ...ruthlessly controlled, it not only ...ided the city, but also split up ...ny families who happened to ...e in different parts of the city.

Teams of workers built the wall at great speed.

A few people were allowed to cross the wall at special checkpoints.

People crossed the ruined wall from East to West after 1989.

In 2009, celebrations marked the 20th anniversary of the fall of the wall.

TIMELINE OF EVENTS

1961	1962–1965	1965–1975	1975–1989
Wire fence	Reinforced wire fence	Concrete wall	Strengthened concrete wall with extra security features

Reunification

The GDR held its first free elections in 1990 and soon the new eastern government was meeting the leaders of West Germany to talk about reunifying Germany into one large nation. This was a huge step for both sides—the East had much to gain, but, having been dogged by poverty for years, would need a lot of financial help from the West if the move was to succeed. But on 3 October 1990 the two governments came to an agreement and East Germany was absorbed into the Federal Republic of Germany.

In the communist GDR, one of the few available cars was the Trabant, a tiny, underpowered vehicle with bodywork made of a kind of plastic.

After reunification, Germans from both parts of the country at last had the chance to get access to western technology and luxury goods.

Trabant

BMW

Schleswig-Holstein

Hamburg

Mecklenburg-Vorpommern

Bremen

Niedersachsen

Berlin

Brandenburg

Sachsen-Anhalt

Nordrhein-Westfalen

G E R M A N Y

Sachsen

Thüringen

Hessen

Rheinland-Pfalz

Saarland

Bayern

Baden-Württemburg

Unified Germany
The new country tha was formed in 1990 had a population of around 80 million an consisted of 16 state in a federation. This i a form of governmer in which power is divided between the states and the centra government.

Deutschmark
The western Deutschmark became the currency of the whole country.

Deutschmark

Turning Point

The fall of the Berlin Wall brought huge changes to Germany. The East gained the freedom brought by western-style democracy and the new united Germany became one of Europe's most prosperous countries. Knocking down the wall was also a signal that communism was coming to an end in eastern and central Europe. By 1990, formerly communist countries such as Hungary, Poland, Romania and Czechoslovakia had removed their old totalitarian governments and were beginning the exciting, but difficult, journey to freedom.

New Germany
Under the flag of the Federal Republic of Germany, the united Germany has become successful. But it took years of investment and hard work to rebuild the damage caused by the communists in the East.

The flag of the Federal Republic of Germany

CELEBRATING REUNIFICATION

Both the fall of the wall and the reunification of Germany were widely celebrated. This crowd is celebrating in front of the Reichstag (German Parliament building) on the day unification took place, 3 October 1990.

PIECES OF WALL

After the much-hated wall was demolished, many people took pieces of it home as souvenirs. Now, fragments are sold to tourists and larger pieces have even been sold at auction.

Indian Ocean Tsunami

On 26 December 2004, the world's biggest recorded earthquake created a huge rip in the seabed beneath the Indian Ocean and was felt thousands of kilometres away. The tear in the seabed caused an enormous tsunami, a tidal wave 15 metres (50 ft) high in places that spread across the ocean, devastating the coasts of countries such as Thailand, Indonesia and Sri Lanka. More than 200,000 people were killed as the tsunami hit Southeast Asia. It was one of the worst natural disasters the world has known.

The earthquake occurred off the coast of Sumatra, Indonesia.

TSUNAMI

A tsunami begins with a huge shock under the sea caused by an earthquake or an erupting volcano. The shock pushes along vast volumes of water, creating a series of waves around 45 minutes apart. The waves can be quite small—only 1 metre (40 in) or so high—in the open ocean, but their height grows dramatically as they near the shore.

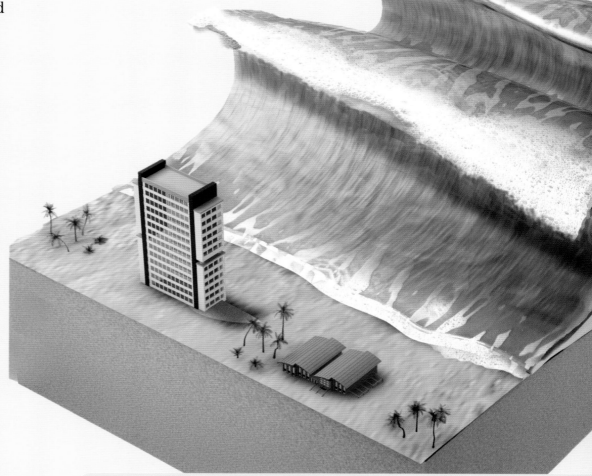

Before the tsunami

The water retreats

Disaster strikes

Monster tsunami

At first, all was calm off Aceh province on the morning of 26 December 2004. Then the water near the coast pulled back towards a growing wave out to sea. Finally, the enormous waves crashed onto the shore.

From earthquake to tsunami

Earthquakes occur along lines of weakness, called faults, in Earth's crust. When the quake strikes, the crust on one side of the fault moves upwards, violently pushing whatever is on top out of the way.

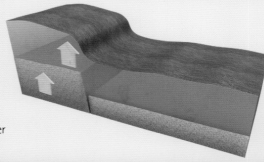

The earthquake h

The energy of earthquake jolts seabed, making surface uneven, li huge step. This pushe the water too, turning ocean's calm surface a churning mass of wa

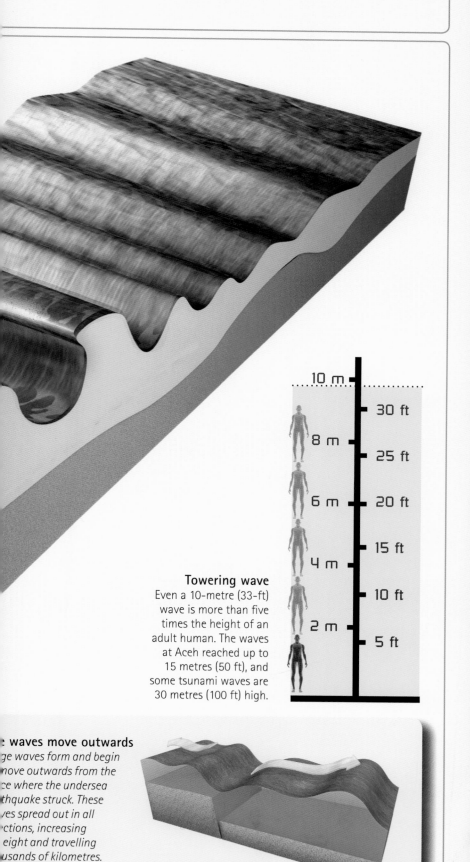

10 m	
8 m	30 ft
	25 ft
6 m	20 ft
	15 ft
4 m	
	10 ft
2 m	5 ft

Towering wave
Even a 10-metre (33-ft) wave is more than five times the height of an adult human. The waves at Aceh reached up to 15 metres (50 ft), and some tsunami waves are 30 metres (100 ft) high.

waves move outwards
ge waves form and begin
move outwards from the
e where the undersea
thquake struck. These
ves spread out in all
ctions, increasing
eight and travelling
usands of kilometres.

Countries Affected

Eleven countries were badly affected by the tsunami. Indonesia was closest to the epicentre of the quake and the island of Sumatra suffered very badly—in some villages near the coast up to 70 per cent of the people were killed. Sri Lanka took a major hit; in Thailand there was a large death toll, which included many tourists as well as local people; and the southeast coast of India was also badly affected. Further afield, the tsunami reached East Africa, and although the casualties there were fewer, many homes on the shore were destroyed.

India
More than 10,000 people were killed in India and hundreds of thousands lost their homes in the destruction. The worst affected area was the state of Tamil Nadu, in the eastern part of India's southern tip.

Sri Lanka
In addition to more than 30,000 deaths, Sri Lanka's agriculture was badly affected, because the spread of salt water ruined fields used to grow rice.

Africa
Although there was some destruction in Somalia, the impact of the tsunami was lessened in Africa because the energy of the waves was reduced by shallow banks in the Indian Ocean. The waves hit Kenya and Tanzania at low tide, also weakening their effect.

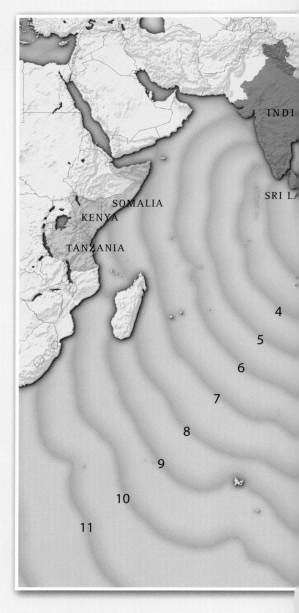

The next day
Banda Aceh is the capital—and largest city—of Indonesia's Aceh province. The coastal fringes of the city show the inundation and damage caused by the tsunami, which hit 24 hours earlier.

GLADESH

YANMAR

THAILAND

MALAYSIA

INDONESIA

A N

A N

Tsunami death toll
- >100 000
- 10 001–100 000
- 1 000–10 000
- <1 000
- Insufficient data

Shock wave
The displacement of the sea floor sent a shock wave racing across the ocean. This map shows the hour-by-hour progress of the wave over 11 hours.

Earthquake epicentre
The epicentre of the earthquake was about 100 kilometres (60 mi) off the coast of Sumatra. From here, the waves fanned out across the globe, reaching Sri Lanka about two hours later and the northwest coast of Australia after four to five hours.

Southeast Asia
In Thailand, more than 5,000 people were killed in the southern provinces facing the Andaman Sea. Other countries in the region, such as Myanmar—formerly Burma—also suffered casualties and damage.

Indonesia
Most of Indonesia's casualties occurred in the province of Aceh, on the island of Sumatra. Rebuilding the flattened towns and villages has taken years and reconstruction continues.

The Tsunami Hits

The tsunami hit with such speed that few people in its path could escape. In some places, there was a "negative wave", making the sea empty before the huge tidal wave struck. Some people who recognised this sign escaped by running to higher ground. But most people near the coast stood no chance. The wave swept away everything from cars to fishing boats, demolished buildings and drowned everyone in its path. The Sumatran city of Banda Aceh, for example, was wiped out by the tsunami. In Indonesia as a whole, some 130,000 people died and half a million became homeless.

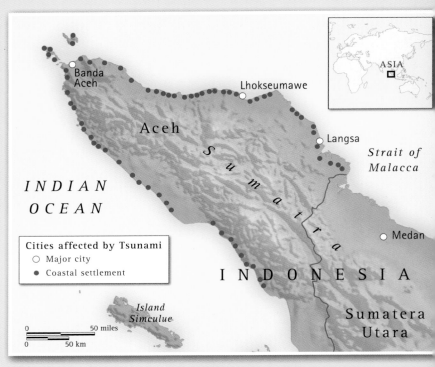

Worst-hit places The northern part of Sumatra was most badly hit. Most people lived in towns and villages along the coast, right in the path of the devastating wave.

Mangroves In the swampy coastal areas in some parts of Sri Lanka and Southeast Asia, the trees have above-ground roots that form dense thickets. These roots helped to protect inland areas from the impact of the wave.

Devastation In Aceh, people who survived the tsunami were faced with huge piles of rubble where their homes once stood. They sifted through the debris to try to salvage possessions that would enable them to carry on their lives.

Warning Systems

TSUNAMI EARLY WARNING SYSTEM

As a result of the disaster, proper tsunami warning systems have been installed to prepare people next time a tsunami occurs in the Indian Ocean. These warning systems are modelled on those already in place in the Hawaii-based Pacific Tsunami Warning Center, which monitors the Pacific. Sensors on the seabed send messages to surface buoys, which relay radio warnings to satellites orbiting Earth. From here, warnings can be sent straight to coastal settlements, where sirens, radio and TV broadcasts, and text messages can alert people in danger areas.

Sea to sky
The data collected by the buoy is sent to a communications satellite orbiting Earth.

Sky to ground
Information from the communications satellite is sent to special ground stations, where civil defence staff read the signals and take action if a tsunami appears to be on the way.

Sea floor to surface
Data from the pressure sensor is transmitted through the water to a buoy floating on the ocean surface. The buoy may also track unusual changes in the height of the water surface.

Tsunameter
A pressure sensor on the seabed detects undersea earthquakes and other changes. It can pick up tremors as small as 1 centimetre (0.4 in), to provide advance warning of larger movements.

Turning Point

The 2004 tsunami was a terrible disaster. As well as the huge death toll, many suffered through injury or because they lost their homes or jobs. Some remote areas have still not recovered from the damage. But the international community made a huge effort to help, bringing in medical aid, providing shelter, rebuilding communities and helping to install warning systems. The world is better prepared for natural disasters as a result.

Warning signs
Many beach areas where tsunamis are likely to occur now have these warning signs. The signs, like this one at Koh Lipe, Thailand, tell people what to do when a tsunami strikes.

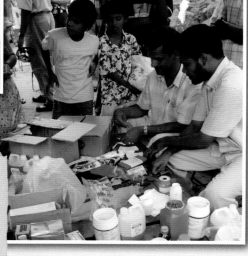

MEDICAL AID

People feared that infections would spread rapidly in the poor conditions faced by tsunami-struck communities. But aid agencies sent doctors to the affected areas, together with supplies of medicines, and this helped reduce the risk of epidemics.

Fatalities This graph shows the approximate numbers of deaths from the 2004 tsunami. The figures represent fatalities confirmed by the government of each country—the total death toll may be higher.

Indonesia 126,900

Sri Lanka 31,000
India 10,700
Thailand 5,400
Somalia 300
Maldives 80
Malaysia 70
Myanmar 60
Tanzania 10
Other* 9

* Other includes Seychelles, Bangladesh, South Africa, Yemen and Kenya.

Timeline

World War I begins
Archduke Franz Ferdinand of Austria is shot dead in Sarajevo, Bosnia. The assassination, by a Bosnian Serb, Gavrilo Princip, begins a worldwide conflict that will become the most devastating war to date.

War ends
Fighting in World War I comes to an end with the defeat of the Central Powers (Austria, Germany and their allies). In 1919, the Treaty of Versailles limits the military power of Germany.

1912

1914

1918

Titanic
The enormous luxurious ocean liner *Titanic*, which some said was unsinkable, collides with an iceberg and sinks on its maiden voyage from Europe to North America.

Humans land on the Moon
The US Apollo 11 spacecraft successfully lands on the Moon. Astronauts Neil Armstrong and Buzz Aldrin do some experiments on the lunar surface and then return safely to Earth.

Space race begins
The Russians launch Sputnik 1, the first artificial satellite to orbit Earth. This tiny satellite begins a race between the USA and the USSR to achieve greater and greater feats of space exploration.

1969

1961

1957

Berlin Wall is built
To prevent contact between the two halves of the city, the East German government orders a wall to be built all the way around the eastern part of Berlin. Armed guards prevent East Germans from escaping to the west.

Berlin Wall falls
After protests on the streets of Berlin, the East German government finally allows people to pass freely through the wall that divides the city. Shortly afterwards, people begin to knock down the wall.

1985

1989

Undersea explorers
Robert Ballard and Jean-Louis Michel locate *Titanic* at the bottom of the ocean. They explore the wreck and bring up items belonging to passengers and crew.

World War II begins
The German army invades Poland and when they refuse to leave, Britain declares war on Germany. More and more countries are drawn into the conflict, which spreads across Europe and beyond.

1937

Hindenburg disaster
The huge *Hindenburg* airship catches fire at Lakehurst, New Jersey. Several people lose their lives as the huge aircraft turns into a fireball; the use of airships for carrying passengers comes to an end.

1939

Pearl Harbor
The Japanese air force bombs the American base at Pearl Harbor, Hawaii, destroying numerous ships. This brings the USA into the war, and their huge military power will eventually help defeat Germany and its allies.

1945

1941

World War II ends
The Allies defeat Germany, bringing peace to Europe in May. When US aircraft drop atomic bombs on two Japanese cities in August, Japan surrenders, ending the war completely.

International Space Station
The construction of this large space station begins. It enables astronauts and scientists from several countries to live in space and do long-term scientific experiments.

Indian Ocean tsunami
On 26 December an enormous earthquake in the Indian Ocean causes a vast tsunami that devastates the coasts of Thailand, Indonesia, Sri Lanka and several other countries. Many are killed and in Indonesia entire communities are wiped out.

1990 1998

2004

Germany is reunited
The two parts of Germany are democratically reunited under the flag of the Federal Republic of Germany. Democracy also returns to neighbouring former communist countries.

Glossary

Allies in World War I, the nations (at first Great Britain and France, and later many others) who opposed the Central Powers; in World War II, those (mainly Great Britain, the USSR and the USA, but also many others) who fought against the Axis Powers.

Alloy a substance made of a mixture of two or more metals, sometimes with the addition of other chemical elements.

Austro-Hungarian Empire the empire made up of the modern countries of Austria and Hungary, plus at various times other territories including Poland, Romania, Bosnia, Serbia and the Czech lands.

Axis the group of countries (Germany, Italy, Japan and other nations) opposed to the Allies in World War II.

Bow the front part of a ship or boat.

Bulkhead a watertight wall in a ship, designed to prevent water from spreading from one part of the vessel to another.

Buoy a float used as a marker in the sea or for carrying signalling equipment.

Capitalist the term used to describe a political system that permits a free market in goods and services, and allows individuals and companies to own businesses.

Central Powers the group of countries (including Germany and the Austro-Hungarian Empire) opposed to the Allies in World War I.

Colony an area of land settled by people from another country and usually governed from that country.

Combatant taking active part in a war.

Command Module the section of the Apollo spacecraft that orbited the Moon and brought the crew back to Earth.

Communist a term used to describe a form of government in which the state owns all industries and has control over the economy, and in which social classes are abolished.

Concentration camp a type of prison in which political prisoners, prisoners of war and others are held, often tortured and in some cases killed.

Cosmonaut the Russian term for an astronaut.

Czar an emperor or ruler of the Russian Empire in the period before 1917.

Czechoslovakia a former country in central Europe east of Germany, made up of the modern Czech Republic and Slovakia.

Dictator a ruler, often a tyrant, who has complete power over the people of his country.

Dominion one of the larger, self-governing countries once part of the British Empire and now part of the Commonwealth of Nations.

Earth's crust the rocks that make up the solid outer surface of Earth; the crust is made up of a number of enormous sections or plates, and it is at the areas where these sections join that earthquakes can occur.

Epicentre the point on Earth's surface that is directly above the focal point of an earthquake.

Fascist a person or state that follows the ideas of fascism—extreme right-wing politics combined with rule by a dictator.

Fault a break or line of weakness in the rocks that make up Earth's crust, where the separate sections of the crust can move, causing earthquakes.

Federal Republic of Germany the official name of the western state of Germany and, after 1990, of the complete, reunified Germany.

Federation a country made up of several separate states, each of which keeps some powers of government.

Flammable capable of catching fire easily.

Free elections elections in which people are free to vote according to their own wishes without interference and in which any political party can take part.

Front a distinct area of combat in a war.

German Democratic Republic the official name of the eastern, communist state of Germany before 1990.

Gothic a style of architecture, popular between the 13th and 15th centuries and again in the 19th century, using pointed arches and stone vaulted ceilings.

Hangar a large shed in which aeroplanes or airships are made and stored.

Headwind a wind blowing the opposite way to the direction of travel of a ship or aircraft, slowing the progress of the craft.

Holocaust the mass killing of Jews and other groups of people such as Gypsies during World World II.

Hull the main body of a ship or boat.

Infrared electromagnetic waves with wavelengths slightly greater than those of visible light and ultraviolet waves.

Jugular vein a large vein in the neck that takes blood from the face and brain to the heart.

Kaiser the title of the emperor or ruler of Germany between 1871 and 1918.

Liner a large ship carrying passengers.

Lunar Module a section of the Apollo spacecraft that landed on the surface of the Moon.

Lunar rover a small, lightweight vehicle specially designed for travel across the surface of the Moon; lunar rovers were used on several of the Apollo missions to the Moon, but not on Apollo 11.

Mangrove a type of tropical tree or shrub that has above-ground or aerial roots; swampy terrain in which these trees or shrubs grow.

Mooring mast a tall vertical structure where an airship was tethered before and after a flight.

Munitions weapons and ammunition used in war.

NASA National Aeronautics and Space Administration, the American organisation that runs the USA's space exploration program.

Nazi the short term for the German National Socialist Party, the extreme right-wing party led by Adolf Hitler before and during World War II.

Negative wave the movement that occurs during a tsunami in which the water moves away from the coast, causing the sea to "empty".

Operation a military action, forming part of a larger war.

Ottoman Empire an empire based in Turkey and lasting from the 14th century until 1922, at its height stretching into eastern Europe and across the eastern Mediterranean to parts of North Africa.

Promenade a deck on a ship or airship designed to give people the space to walk around and admire the view.

Reception room on a ship, a space designed for the use of a large number of passengers as a sitting room or for group social functions.

Regime the system of government of a country or state.

Right-wing a political term describing a person or party with conservative views.

Rudder a device, made up of a flat movable plate, used to steer a ship, boat or aircraft.

Satellite an object that orbits a planet such as Earth. The Moon is a satellite, but there are also artificial satellites, made and sent into space by humans.

Seismometer a device used to measure movements in Earth's surface.

Sensor a device that responds to a particular kind of wave or movement—a solar sensor responds to the Sun's light, a movement sensor can respond to earth tremors.

Service Module a section of the Apollo spacecraft that housed engines, fuel and other items, and which was attached to the Command Module until it was jettisoned before re-entry to Earth's atmosphere at the end of the mission.

Ship's officers people doing the most senior jobs on a ship, such as the Captain, First Officer and Chief Engineer.

Sortie the flight of a military aircraft forming part of a mission during a war.

Space agency an organisation that runs a programme of space exploration.

Stage a section of a rocket, designed so that it can be detached from the spacecraft when it has been used.

Stasi the short name for the East German Ministry of State Security, a secret police organisation.

Stoker a person whose job it is to keep a ship's engine supplied with fuel.

Submersible a small submarine, sometimes one that can be operated by remote control from the surface of the water.

Totalitarian a term used to describe a state or government that uses ruthless authority to impose extreme political views on its people.

Treaty a formal agreement or pact between two countries or states, often setting down the terms of peace after a war.

Trench warfare a form of warfare in which the two sides occupy long parallel trenches and one side tries to capture the trench of the enemy and the land behind it.

Ultraviolet type of electromagnetic waves with wavelengths slightly greater than those of visible violet light.

USSR an abbreviation for the Union of Soviet Socialist Republics, the vast communist state made up of Russia and neighbouring areas that existed from 1922 to 1991.

Weightless the effect of the low gravity on the Moon, where gravity is only about one-sixth as strong as that on Earth.

Index

Credits

KEY: ALA = Alamy, ASM = Smithsonian Air and Space Museum, AWM = Australian War Memorial, CBT = Corbis, ESA = European Space Ag, GI = Getty, HSK = Honeysucklecreek.net, IS = iStock Photo, MP = Minden Pictures, N = NASA, NOAA = National Oceanic and Atmospheric Administration, TPL = The Photo Library, PD = Public Domain, SH = Shutterstock, PD = Picture Desk, TF = Top Foto

PHOTOGRAPHS: 1cc TPL; 3b TPL; 4bl, bc, cr GI; 5cl NSM, cr TF; 6cl PIC, cr TPL; 7cl, br TPL; 8cc, cl TPL; 9bl, t TPL; 11cl, tl ALA; cl CBT; 11b, c CBT, c GI, c NOAA; 13cc, bc TPL cl, bl iS, cl CBT; 14cl GI, cr TPL; 15cc, cc CBT; 16br AWM, b CBT; 17b CBT, b GI, b PUB; 19tr CBT; c GI; 20cc, cl CBT, br GI; 21 tl PUB, cc IS, cc GI, bc CBT; 22bl GI; 24c CBT; 25t CBT; 26bc, bc, br TF; 27bc, br, bl TF; 28c CBT, b GI, cl PUB, bl TPL; 29 cl iScl TPL, b SH 30bc CBT, cl, c CBT, tl GI; 31c CBT; 32bc, bl CBT; 33bc, bl, br CBT; 34cl CBT; 36tl GI, c, bl CBT; 37 cl CBT, c GI, cl iS; 38tr ASM, cl, bc N; 40tl ASM, cr CBT, br N; 41c ASM, b CBT, b N, c, c, t TPL; 42br, br, cr HSK, tr NSM; 43c, tr N; 44c, c, br N; 45c, c N, bl ESA; 46bc TF; 47tr, bl TF; 48tl TF; 49c, tr TF; 50tl PUB, b TF; 51c GI, bl, br CBT, b, b TF; 52c, c TF, bl PUB; 53c TF, cr IS, b CBT; 57c CBT; 58bl MP, br CBT; 59c, tr CBT; 60tl CBT; 61c, c CBT, bl IS; 62tl, tc, CBT, tl TPL, bc NOAA; bl TF; 63tc, cl, c, bc CBT, bl TF.

ILLUSTRATIONS: Front cover Malcolm Godwin/Moonrunner Design; Francesca D'Ottavi/ Wilkinson Studios 18b; Godd.com 22–23, 29cr, 34–35, 40cbl, 46–7, 54b, 55b, 62c; Leonello Calvetti 4tl, 6–7, 8b, 11br; Iain McKellar 10–11b; Library of Congress 4cl, 7tc; Malcolm Godwin/ Moonrunner Design 5b, 26–7, 54–55, 63tl, br; Peter Bull Art Studio 9br; 10–11, 48–9, 54–5b, 60; Steve Hobbs 38–39, 40b, 42–3, 45tl.